3

Cape Ann

a photographic portrait

Photography by Alan Murtagh

Narrative by Sara Day

SECOND EDITION

First published in the United States of
America by:

Twin Lights Publishers, Inc.
8 Hale Street
Rockport, Massachusetts 01966
Telephone: (978) 546-7398
http://www.twinlightspub.com

ISBN: 978-1-934907-09-2
ISBN: 1-934907-09-X

10 9 8 7 6 5 4 3 2 1

Singing Beach (*opposite*)
Frothy waves sweep the shore along Singing
Beach in Manchester-by-the-Sea. This charming
and popular beach gets its name from the subtle
squeaking sound of the sand as you walk along.

(*jacket front*)
Farmhouse reflected in calm waters
Essex, MA

(*frontispiece*)
Sailing past Straitsmouth Island Lighthouse
Rockport, MA

(*jacket back, clockwise from top left*)
Fisherman's Memorial, Gloucester, MA
Motif #1, Rockport, MA
Tuck's Point, Manchester-by-the-Sea, MA
Sailing Dory, Essex, MA

Book design by:
SYP Design & Production, Inc.
www.sypdesign.com

Printed in China

A Place in the Heart

You can feel it in the soft sands of Wingaersheek Beach, hear it in the thundering waves of the Back Shore, and smell it in the crisp, salty air that permeates the region. It's the heart of a place that beats with rustic beauty. It's the heart of Cape Ann.

Gloucester, Rockport, Essex, and Manchester-by-the-Sea are the brilliant gems that make the treasure of New England sparkle. From the historic fishing industry to the creative art colonies, Cape Ann is a place like no other. And with its traditional festivals, incredible seafood, overflowing antique shops, and scenic splendor, it's no wonder the area draws thousands of visitors each year.

In perfect step with the striking beauty of this place, are the people who make it their home. Creative, stalwart, as solid as the granite they stand on, the people of Cape Ann are the salt of the earth. Living their lives by the rhythm of the seasons, they are quick to share food, friendship, and a plethora of stories with a tried-and-true "Yankee" spirit.

Photographer Alan Murtagh has been capturing the beauty of this unique place for 15 years. His images evoke the spirit of Cape Ann in a way that stirs the viewer's imagination—you not only see it, you can actually *sense* it.

When you come to Cape Ann, you'll soon discover it's not just a visit, it's an experience. And when you leave here, you never really leave, because Cape Ann is a place in the heart.

— Sara Day

View from the Headlands

Sailboats dot the horizon on a serene afternoon. A couple finds the Headlands in Rockport a peaceful place to take in a generous slice of summer.

THEY THAT GO
DOWN TO THE SEA
IN SHIPS
▲   ▲   ▲
1623 — 1923

Gloucester Fisherman's Memorial *(left)*

With a firm hand on the wheel and a steady gaze toward the harbor and beyond, the "Man at the Wheel," located on Stacy Boulevard, has become a symbol of the City of Gloucester. Created by Leonard Craske in 1925, the bronze icon of courage and strength is a tribute to the thousands of mariners who lost their lives at sea.

Fisherman's Wives Memorial *(above)*

Sculpted by Morgan Faulds Pike in 2001, the Fisherman's Wives Memorial depicts the strength of fishing families everywhere. At the base is an inscription that reads: "The wives, mothers, daughters and sisters of Gloucester fishermen honor the wives and families of fishermen and mariners everywhere for their faith, diligence, and fortitude."

Tarr and Wonson Paint Factory

This cluster of red buildings at the end of the Rocky Neck peninsula was built over 140 years ago. Though feeling its age, the Tarr and Wonson Paint Factory is still standing, much to the delight of artists who flock to capture it on canvas. The Ocean Alliance is an organization dedicated to taking steps in restoring this historic site.

An Open House

James G. Tarr and Augustus H. Wonson invented copper-based marine paint which made boats less susceptible to harsh Atlantic waters. The historic building where the paint was manufactured was purchased in 2008 by Ocean Alliance. To raise restoration awareness, The Paint Factory opened its doors for a one-time tour and art show.

Gloucester City Hall

Built in 1871 and designed by Boston architects Gridley J. F. Bryant and Louis P. Rogers, Gloucester City Hall has recently undergone an extensive historic renovation. Along with government offices, the building houses a Fishermen's Memorial as well as official documents from the 1600s. City Hall is included in the National Register of Historic Places.

Art, History, and Culture

From fishing ports to granite quarries, the history of Cape Ann is extensively documented here at the Cape Ann Museum. The fine art collection includes prominent American artists such as Winslow Homer, Edward Hopper, and Fitz Henry (Hugh) Lane who have so eloquently captured Cape Ann. Located on Pleasant Street, the museum is opened Tuesday through Sunday.

Ten Pound Island *(opposite)*

The history of this scenic island includes sightings of a large sea serpent during the 1800s. In the summer of 1880, American artist Winslow Homer stayed on the island and created over 50 Gloucester Harbor paintings. The original 30-foot tower was built in 1881 and is still actively navigating ships in and out of the harbor.

Strolling Main Street

(above, left, and opposite)

Gloucester's Main Street is a celebration for the senses, beginning with the long-established Virgilio's Italian bakery at the West end. Specialty boutiques, great restaurants, and eclectic galleries line the street and spill over to adjoining side streets as well. While the basic row architecture has remained the same, the faces of the shops have undergone numerous colorful changes throughout the years.

Sargent House Museum

Built in 1782 for writer and women's rights advocate Judith Sargent Murray, the Sargent House depicts Gloucester's early history. Home to sea merchants and prominent leaders, its rooms are decorated with period furnishings and walls are adorned with paintings by famous American artist John Singer Sargent, descendant of the Sargent family.

The Old Blackburn Tavern

Stranded at sea in a dory in the winter of 1883, Howard Blackburn wrapped his fingers around both oars and rowed to safety. All of his fingers, frozen in a cupped position from gripping the oars, were lost to frostbite. Unable to remain a fisherman, Blackburn opened a saloon on this site in 1886. It was a great success with the townspeople. The building now houses Halibut Point restaurant, a fine establishment that shares the same success today.

Gloucester Stage Company

The Gloucester Stage Company has been presenting outstanding play productions since its founding in 1979. GSC has received much notoriety, including Boston's Elliot Norton Prize awarded to cofounder and playwright Israel Horovitz.

Schooner Race

The Mayor's Race is part of the annual Gloucester Schooner Festival, an event that pays tribute to classic fishing schooners that contributed so much to this oldest seaport. Spectacular tall ships under full sail are a thrilling sight to see. In the evening, a lighted boat parade cruises through the Annisquam River and out into the harbor.

Cleaning the Nets *(above)*

It seems as if this seagull "foreman" has his team well under control as he delegates the tending of a fishing net. Gill net fishing is popular throughout New England. Gill nets are devised to catch fish by trapping them in the mesh. When they find they cannot squeeze through, they try backing out, but their gills get caught in the mesh.

Maritime Dreamer *(opposite)*

Colorful, docked fishing vessels conjure up dreams of high-sea adventures for a young potential sailor.

Trawlers in Port *(above)*

Western Sea Fishing Company's three large mid-water trawlers, *Endeavor*, *Challenger*, and *Voyager* are docked in calm waters. These massive vessels fish for mackerel and herring and can hold hundreds of thousands of pounds of fish.

Salting Herring *(left)*

Fresh herring is salted as it pours down a shoot and into a barrel. Many lobster fishermen use herring for bait. Salting the fish preserves them for those times when the herring is in short supply.

Water Color Reflections

Though bright and varied, these gentle, fluid colors are in sharp contrast to the harsh lifestyle of the commercial fishing industry they reflect. These vessels are safe at home in this serene scene, but rough seas and frigid temperatures are all part of the job.

Telling It Like It Is

Definitive of the local color of Cape Ann, this tag line says it all. Founded in 1979, Cape Ann Tuna is a wholesale tuna company located on Parker Street at the State Fish Pier.

Tugboat in Dock

The bright colors of a tugboat demand attention, but the dockworkers in the background remain focused on their respective tasks at hand. Vessel maintenance is an ongoing undertaking on the waterfront.

Textures of the Waterfront *(opposite)*

Here in Gloucester, there is something wonderfully creative in the air that can turn ordinary objects into objects d'art. A simple line laid on a dock creates an abstract masterpiece – a true work of art which, through color, texture, and shape, defines the very essence of this waterfront community.

Cruiseport (above)

With architecture that evokes the spirit of a great ship, Cruiseport Gloucester is an impressively elegant venue with a luxurious ballroom for weddings and events. The Gloucester Marine Terminal, also here at Cruiseport, accommodates large ships up to 500 feet, dockside. And if it's great seafood you're craving, you'll find it at Cruiseport's Seaport Grill.

Gloucester Waterfront Festival (right)

Every summer, over 175 artists and artisans display their works along historic Stage Fort Park at the Gloucester Waterfront Festival. Crafts, folk art, live music, gourmet jams and jellies, ethnic foods, and a New England clam bake draw thousands of visitors every year.

Multi-purpose Harbor (opposite)

Enormous cruise ships share the inner harbor with huge tankers and fishing vessels of various sizes. Thanks to the Terminal Marina at Cruiseport that opened in 2007, Gloucester is now a vacationer's port of call. Visitors from all over the world come to explore the oldest fishing community in the country.

Chebacco Boat *(top)*

Named for Chebacco Parish, once part of Ipswich, these small sturdy boats were popular in the 1800s. Their small size, with an average 30-foot deck, made it a suitable craft for a small fishing crew. Many of these schooners met their demise during the War of 1812, when they were an easy target for the Royal Navy.

Eastern Point Lighthouse *(bottom)*

The first lighthouse on Eastern Point was a 30-foot-tall stone tower built in 1832. Her keeper, Samuel Wonson, was paid $400 yearly. In 1848, a new 34-foot lighthouse was built. French red plate glass dubbed it the "ruby light." It was replaced in 1890 by the present 36-foot tower which remains an active navigational aid today.

Dog Bar Breakwater *(opposite)*

Built between 1894 and 1905 by the Army Corp of Engineers, the Dog Bar Breakwater stretches 2,250 feet in front of the Eastern Point Lighthouse. Whether strolling along the great granite blocks or spending an afternoon casting a line, it is an exhilarating spot. At the tip of the breakwater is a light that marks the dangerous Dog Bar Reef.

Half Moon Beach *(opposite)*

A hidden gem in Stage Fort Park is Half Moon Beach. Calm and quiet, it's a tiny stretch of sand with clear water and beautiful harbor views. Surrounded by shady cliffs, it is a respite from the hot sun on a summer day. A natural water park, children delight in swimming out to the smooth rocks, climbing up, and jumping off.

Granite Pathways *(above)*

Granite stairs and pathways make their way throughout the huge granite boulders of the Stage Fort Park waterfront. Follow them to discover Half Moon Beach or military cannons from the War of 1812. Or hike up them to the top of Tablet Rock, for an outstanding view of the busy harbor and the surrounding city.

Calm Waters *(above)*

A Navy ship heads out along the horizon of a calm harbor in the glow of a glorious sunrise viewed from Stage Fort Park. The park was once a fort with cannons strategically placed within the hills to guard against pirates and enemy warships during the War of 1812.

Parade of Lights *(opposite)*

Vessels large and small light up the night during the Parade of Lights as part of the Gloucester Schooner Festival. The grand spectacle meanders down the Annisquam River and makes its way into the harbor. Spectators participate with flashlights and glowsticks along the route. The evening ends with a spectacular fireworks display.

Stage Fort Park (above)

Overlooking the harbor, this beautiful plot of land is the site of the founding of the Massachusetts Bay Colony. Nestled in the hills are historic cannons that echo the days of the War of 1812. Today, it's a peaceful meeting place for picnics, baseball, or a summer concert. Stage Fort Park is part of the Essex National Heritage Area.

Small-Town Patriotism (left)

In a show of patriotism, Old Glory is displayed prominently along a long stretch of waterfront. To celebrate the 4th of July, summer visitors and residents gather along Stacy Boulevard to watch the impressive fireworks over Gloucester Harbor.

Teamwork *(above)*

The crew of the *Nina* sets out for a practice session for the hugely anticipated St. Peter's Fiesta Seine Boat Race. In a true test of strength, three 12-member crews—each made up of 10 rowers, a helmsman, and a coxswain—compete in a grueling mile-long race that begins and ends on the shore of Pavilion Beach.

Seine Boat Tradition *(right)*

These large, sturdy boats were used by fishermen in earlier days to set out nets and haul fish onto a larger vessel. Since the fishing fleet was in port during the St. Peter's Fiesta, seine boats were available for racing. The days of seining are gone, but these boats are still used today as part of the long-standing tradition of the fiesta.

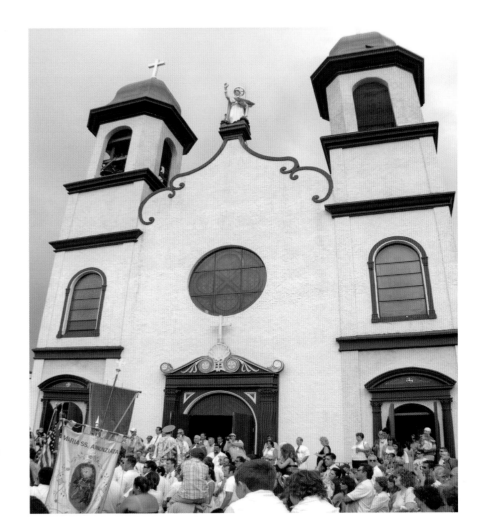

Our Lady of Good Voyage

The Portuguese community of Gloucester joins their Sicilian counterparts during the St. Peter's Fiesta and honors Our Lady of Good Voyage. At the top of Our Lady of Good Voyage Church, the protective Blessed Mother cradles a fishing vessel in her arms.

Top That!

Color and creativity abound during this highly popular religious festival. A fiesta reveler balances the many aspects of the celebration atop her head.

Viva, San Pietro! *(opposite top and bottom)*

In 1927, a Sicilian fisherman, Captain Salvatore Favazza, commissioned a Boston sculptor to create a statue of St. Peter, the patron saint of fishermen. Since that time, the saint has been honored with a four-day celebration that includes boat races, a greasy pole contest, a colorful parade, and the gathering of boats in the harbor for the blessing of the fleet. The fiesta draws thousands to the city every summer.

Gloucester's Back Shore

Crashing waves cascade from a large granite boulder in an impressive display along Gloucester's "Back Shore." These rocks are often a resting spot for gulls and cormorants. A drive along Atlantic Road during a storm is a great way to observe the raw power and fury of the Atlantic Ocean. It is one of the most scenic stretches of road in New England.

Fitz Henry Lane *(top)*

Born in 1804, Gloucester native Fitz Henry (Hugh) Lane was one of America's most famous maritime artists. Stricken with polio from childhood, he was a master of luminism—his paintings bathed in glowing light. Created by Alfred Duca, a statue of the artist overlooks the harbor from Duncan's Point, where Lane made his home.

Swan Song *(bottom)*

Mother nature creates a masterpiece all her own as sunlight filters through the feathers of a mature swan. The splendid, natural light during the golden hour is a hallmark of Cape Ann and is what has been drawing artists to the area for years.

Maritime History *(above and left)*

Since 1999, Gloucester Maritime Heritage Center, on Harbor Loop, has been an outstanding resource for learning about the history of Gloucester's fishing fleet and the industries that support it. It consists of the oldest maritime railway in the country along with a boatbuilding shop, educational center, and the Gorton's Seafood Gallery.

Chart Your Course for GMHC

Gorton's Seafood Gallery at the Gloucester Maritime Heritage Center has the ambience of an old wharf warehouse. It features exhibits and artifacts including ship models, foghorns, and sail-making tools. Outside is a hands-on aquarium with plants and sea creatures found throughout the rocky crags and sandy shores of Cape Ann.

Rocky Neck (above)

Art galleries, fabulous eateries, and colorful homes line the narrow, winding roads of historic Rocky Neck. From a fish packing plant, to a sail loft, and then an art gallery, this building now houses The Rudder—a popular restaurant with a reputation for serving some of the very best seafood on Cape Ann.

North Shore Arts Association

(left and opposite)

For over 80 years, the North Shore Arts Association has exhibited the work of North Shore painters and sculpters. With over 300 members, the association also offers demonstrations, workshops, lectures, concerts, films, and children's classes. Located on Pirates Lane, overlooking the inner harbor, they are open from May through October.

An Artist's Haven *(top)*

For fine arts, photography, crafts, and more, the Rocky Neck Art Colony is one of the oldest working art colonies in the country. Drawn by the beauty of the inner harbor and Smith's Cove, artists have been living and working here for over 150 years. Some notable artists who painted here are Emile Gruppé, Winslow Homer, and Childe Hassam.

Colorful Locale *(bottom and opposite)*

Blooming with activity, Rocky Neck is an artsy and eclectic neighborhood located in East Gloucester. Residents enjoy the activity in Smith's Cove year round, while summer tourists flock to the area, by car or by boat, to visit the shops and galleries or to enjoy the delectable seafood restaurants.

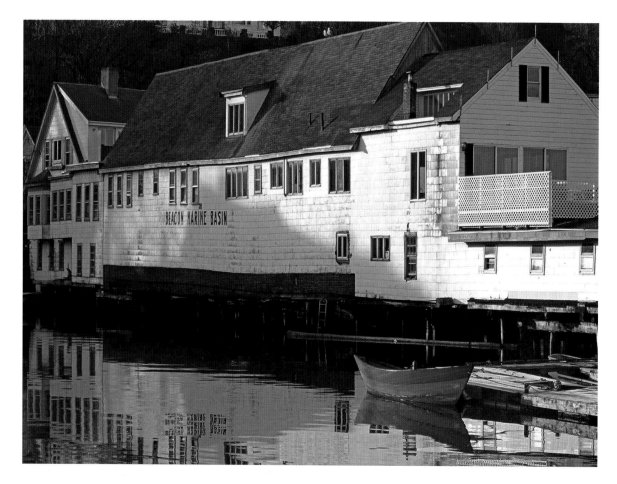

Beacon Marine Basin (*opposite top*)

The weathered structure that is the Beacon Marine Basin building sags comfortably over Smith's Cove in East Gloucester. Over the years, Beacon Marine has filled a number of needs including apartments, a boat yard, a marina, a sail loft, and an art gallery.

Beauport (*opposite bottom*)

On a picture-perfect location, overlooking Gloucester Harbor, Beauport was once home to famous American interior designer, Henry Davis Sleeper. After his death, it was purchased by Charles and Helena McCann, who decided to keep all of Sleeper's art and collectables untouched. Visitors are welcome to veiw them from June through October.

Moon Over Good Harbor (*above*)

The shimmering reflection of moonlight upon a calm and quiet ocean paints a quintessential romantic scene. One of the most popular beaches north of Boston, Good Harbor is a half-mile stretch of smooth sand flanked by a granite coast. Sand dunes protect a fragile salt marsh from which the tide flows in and out via a winding creek.

A Day at the Beach

A warm summer day draws hundreds of beachgoers, but there's plenty of room for everyone on the half-mile stretch of Good Harbor Beach. The beach features a tidal creek that can be a calmer experience for boogie-board loungers. Children also enjoy filling their pails with crabs and minnows along the creek.

Wingaersheek Beach

In West Gloucester, along Ipswich Bay, there is a stunning beach with picturesque views and kid-friendly shores. Families flock to Wingaersheek Beach for its wide-open area and calm waters. It's a great place to spend a relaxing day, watching the boats sail up and down the Annisquam River.

Catch'n a Wave *(opposite)*

Surf's up at Good Harbor Beach, and these enthusiasts are quick to take advantage of what the mighty Atlantic rolls at them. It's not uncommon to see surfers enjoying the swells here year round, donning wetsuits to guard against the chilly waters of Cape Ann.

Hammond Castle Museum

In 1929, John Hays Hammond, Jr. built this medieval castle in Magnolia, over-looking Gloucester Harbor. It houses his extensive collection of Renaissance art and artifacts. With over 400 patents, Hammond, one of America's most im-portant inventors, was the inventor of remote control by radio waves.

Manchester Bath and Tennis Club

For more than 90 years, the Manchester Bath and Tennis Club has provided its members with great summer recreation, including tennis, private beachfront, a swimming pool, and a full social calendar. The club is located on Magnolia Beach, also known as Gray Beach, which is part of the Coolidge Reservation.

Magnolia Villa

A quaint village of Gloucester, bordering Manchester-by-the-Sea, Magnolia has some of the most stunning ocean-front views on Cape Ann. A community all its own, it was originally established as Kettle Cove in the 1640s, and was renamed for the endangered Sweet-bay Magnolia trees that can be found throughout nearby Ravenswood Park.

Annisquam Yacht Club

Just south of the entrance to Ipswich Bay is the Annisquam Yacht Club. Since 1896, members of this private club have enjoyed its well-protected moorings and excellent location here on the Annisquam River. Members also enjoy tennis and social gatherings. Though a private venue, the club does offer a limited number of guest moorings.

Dinner on the Bridge *(opposite)*

Each year, the Annisquam Village Seafair features its popular "Dinner on the Bridge." Tables are set along the narrow bridge that stretches out over Lobster Cove. A succulent lobster (or chicken) dinner is served to benefit the Annisquam Village Hall Association. The Seafair features food, games, arts and crafts, and more.

Life in the Village *(above)*

Annisquam Village is a small hamlet between Gloucester and Rockport with some of the most quaint and picturesque neighborhoods on Cape Ann. Established in 1631, it was once a community of fishermen and ship builders. The name *Annisquam* is derived from the Indian word "squam" that means harbor and "Ann" for Cape Ann.

New England Charm (above)

With the cyclical change of the seasons, weathered shingles create rich colors that are quintessentially New England, as this front doorway reveals. They are a reminder of the long, harsh winter that gives way to a warmer, gentler spring and summer.

Lanes Cove (opposite top)

Sea kayakers venture out into Ipswich Bay from Lanes Cove. Located in Lanesville, a small village of Gloucester, the cove is protected by a huge, granite breakwater that was once used for loading granite onto boats during the late 1800s and early 1900s. Lanesville is an eclectic community where many creative artists come to settle.

Thacher Island (opposite bottom)

Thacher Island was named for Anthony and Elizabeth Thacher, survivors of a shipwreck in 1635. A National Historic Landmark, the island's two 124-foot-tall, granite lighthouses mark a dangerous stretch of coast. The island's southern end is owned by the Town of Rockport, while the northern end is owned by the U.S. Fish and Wildlife Service.

Perfect for Painting (above)

An artist takes advantage of a picture-perfect day to capture Motif #1 and Rockport Harbor. This little red fishing shack is said to be one of the most painted and photographed buildings in the country. It was dubbed "Motif #1" by artist Lester Hornby because it was the premier subject matter for local artists to paint—and the name stuck.

Motif #1 (opposite)

Colorful buoys, each belonging to a departed lobsterman, dot the side of Motif #1 as tall masts and roof tops reflect the suns last rays of light. The iconic fishing shack was destroyed in the infamous "blizzard of '78" when rough seas and heavy winds swept it from the granite pier. An identical structure was built the same year.

Bearskin Neck (top and opposite)

According to Rockport lore, Ebenezer Babson slew a bear using only his fishing knife, and, thus, saved his young nephew's life. Fishermen spied the bearskin that he laid out on the rocks to dry, and dubbed this parcel of land "Bearskin Neck." The sign above the Pewter Shop tells the story of Ebenezer and the fate of the bear.

Something for Everyone (bottom)

From fine gifts of The Pewter Shop to the delectable aromas of Helmut's Strudel Shop, there is no better place on Cape Ann for strolling and window shopping than Rockport's Bearskin Neck. The narrow alleyway of shops, galleries, and restaurants culminates with a stunning view of Sandy Bay and the Atlantic Ocean beyond.

Small Town International

An afternoon is well spent, strolling the galleries and shops of Rockport's Main Street. One of dozens of interesting shops is La Provence, offering French textiles and fragrances in the form of decorative table cloths and other kitchen staples, as well as delicately scented soaps and lotions.

Dock Square

The meeting point of Main Street, Mount Pleasant Street, and Bearskin Neck, Dock Square is the center of activity in the Town of Rockport. It was in this square that Hannah Jumper and her followers organized a successful protest for temperance in the community back in 1856.

Downtown Rockport *(opposite, top and bottom)*

Rockport is well known for the history of its fishing and quarry industries, however, it is often defined by its extensive arts community that produces a huge scope of exquisite paintings, sculpture, jewelry, and more. At the studio/gallery of Eileen Mueller, visitors browse a collection of paintings that convey an array of moods so inspired by the region.

Inside and Out

Motif #1 is framed by a window pane of one of the many exclusive shops in downtown Rockport. It is a remarkable setting in which to choose that perfect gift, keepsake, or afternoon tea. Not your typical boutiques, Rockport merchants offer quality, creative goods that can satisfy the most discerning shopper.

Inner Harbor Palette

Awash with color, this inner harbor scene takes on the life of a spilled artist's palette. A local fisherman, quietly securing his dory, seems oblivious to the noise of color that surrounds him.

Rockport Public Library *(opposite)*

This solid granite structure on School Street was once the site of the Annisquam Steam Cotton Mill in the 1800s. During the early and mid 20th century, it was the George Tarr Elementary School. Today, it is the Rockport Public Library, with all the modern conveniences, a searchable online catalog, book club, events, and a childrens' story hour.

Summer Gardens *(top)*

Hardy pansies join a chorus of counterparts to sing a song of summer. Colorful gardens lie in wait during long winter months, and burst in radiant abundance throughout this charming seaside village.

Hannah Jumper House *(bottom)*

Fed up with excessive drinking in Rockport, in 1856, Hannah Jumper organized a raid in which she and her like-minded followers vandalized homes and establishments, hatcheting dozens of barrels of liquor in protest of intemperance. One of Rockport's most famous historic events, it deemed Rockport a dry town for nearly 150 years.

The Paper House

Amateur inventor, Elis F. Stenman, began building a house out of newspaper in 1922. Still standing almost 90 years later, the Paper House in Pigeon Cove not only has walls of paper, but furniture as well—even a piano. The Paper House is open each day from spring through fall.

Bursts of Color

Occasional bursts of color make for a pleasant stroll along Rockport's picturesque waterfront.

The Old Castle

While the origin of the name "The Old Castle" is unclear, this 1700s saltbox-style home, in Pigeon Cove, is believed to be one of the oldest buildings on Cape Ann. Jethro Wheeler owned it in the early 1700s, and his family continued to occupy it for the next 6 generations. Open to the public, it is maintained by the Sandy Bay Historical Society.

Cooling Off

Part of the fun of growing up on Cape Ann is taking advantage of a cool, still quarry on a hot summer afternoon. Filled with spring water and rain, quarries can be found in Rockport's private wooded areas.

Curtis Quarry

During the early 20th century, these were active granite quarries. Quarrymen used dynamite to separate huge sections of ledge. Granite slabs were initially carted off by oxen and later by flat rail cars. Today, these deep chasms are filled with fresh water that reflects the gem-like colors of the seasons—emerald in summer; sapphire in winter.

Granite Pier

Granite Pier was used by the Rockport Granite Company to transport huge amounts of high-grade granite to some very famous building sites from Boston's Custom Tower to the Panama Canal. Today, it serves as a boat launch area. The pier will soon undergo repair from damage done by the pounding surf of recent winter storms.

Tall Ship Formidable *(top and bottom)*

The tall ship *Formidable* provides a unique sailing tour experience. The Pirate King (the captain) and crew delight passengers with age-old stories while sailing along on the historic waters of Cape Ann.

Jolly Roger Flying at Dusk *(opposite)*

Her starboard side awash in golden sunlight, the *Formidable* awaits her next excursion at Tuna Wharf on Bearskin Neck.

First Congregational Church *(opposite)*

At the corner of School and Main Streets is the First Congregational Church of Rockport. In 1814, this historic building was the target of a British frigate during the War of 1812. A shot was fired and missed the church bell that was ringing to alarm the town. The Old Sloop Coffeehouse also operates in the church's Fellowship Hall.

Keystone Bridge *(top)*

It took 4 years to clear the area that spans the Keystone Bridge, but only 11 weeks to build the bridge itself. The Rockport Granite Company cut the pathway so that rail cars could more efficiently transport stone from the quarry to the pier.

Rockport Golf Club *(bottom)*

Established as the Rockport Country Club in 1913, this course makes for a great round with wide open play. The elevated clubhouse offers stunning views of Sandy Bay and Thacher Island, as well as a view of the entire course. The club is semi-private with over 300 members.

Halibut Point State Park

The massive quarry at Halibut Point State Park is lined with the same smooth granite that was excavated back in the early 20th century for use in many buildings, bridges, and breakwaters. The Visitor's Center is a 60-foot-tall, WWII fire tower that offers spectacular views that stretch from Ipswich Bay, to New Hampshire, and Maine.

Fiery Sunset

The end of a Cape Ann day boasts a painted sky in breathtaking tones of orange, purple, and gold. Some of the most stunning sunsets on Earth occur at Halibut Point State Park. A favorite attraction on Cape Ann, the scenic park is maintained by the Department of Conservation and Recreation and the Trustees of Reservations.

Still Waters Run Deep

Halibut Point is made of granite sheets that are some 440 million years old. This fresh-water quarry is the former Babson Farm granite quarry that was part of the thriving granite industry of the 19th and early 20th centuries. Rockport granite has been used to construct many famous buildings including a portion of the base of the Statue of Liberty.

4th of July *(top and bottom)*

Not to be outdone by a fancy fireworks display, the Town of Rockport hosts an Independence Day bonfire that is second to none. Held each year at Back Beach, the wildly popular event features a towering stack of wooden pallets that is traditionally topped with an old outhouse and set ablaze at dusk. View it by land or by sea.

Quiet Harbor *(opposite)*

A familiar silhouette is traced against a dramatic sky. With each day offering up scenic wonders such as this, it's no wonder that this small seaport attracts so many artists and art lovers.

Heading Out *(above)*

A lobster boat heads out for the catch of the day. The freshest seafood in New England is hauled in by many of these hard-working "farmers of the sea." Cape Ann restaurants are always filled with satisfied tourists and locals who know that the sweetest flavors come from the coldest Atlantic waters.

Sandy Bay Yacht Club *(left and opposite)*

Rocking chairs at the Sandy Bay Yacht Club are a great way to relax after a brisk day on the ocean. Since 1885, the yacht club has been teaching the art of sailing to youngsters and adults. Sailors participate in weekend races as well as annual regattas. The club also has an active social calendar including cookouts, dances, and pot luck suppers.

Old Harbor (above)

Like a painting brought to life, Old Harbor reflects the surrounding village in waters smooth as a black pearl. Wharfs of huge granite line the deep water inlet. The scene has remained virtually unchanged for years.

Mirrored Motif (left)

Used by Rockport's harbor masters for storing gear, this crimson shed on Granite Pier is a convincing replica of Motif #1. Granite Pier was once an industrious wharf, used by the Rockport Granite Company (1865–1933) to transport massive quarried stones to building sites all across the country.

Old Garden Beach (*above*)

A short walk from town, Old Garden Beach is an intimate stretch of sand with beautiful ocean views. Children love to spend the day discovering small crabs among the rocky, seaweed-laden shoreline.

Memorial Day (*right*)

From Beech Grove Cemetery to Harvey Park, the Rockport Memorial Day Parade makes stops throughout the town to honor all veterans, laying wreaths at commemorative markers along the way. Here, among a crowd of onlookers, the parade gathers at Lumber Wharf to honor the many who lost their lives at sea.

Paddling Pristine Coastline (opposite)

Sea kayakers paddle their way along a unique sight-seeing tour of Rockport. Exploring the rocky coast and islands by sea kayak is a popular activity that tourists and residents can take advantage of from spring to mid-fall. Whether by bike, on foot, or by sea, visiting this pristine New England town is an experience to be treasured.

Till the Next Catch (top)

A lone lobster boat waits to collect her next catch. It's hard to fathom that this delicacy we enjoy today was considered "poverty food" during colonial times. Lobster was so plentiful, it was fed only to prisoners and servants.

Quintessential Rockport (bottom)

Strolling through the small town streets and alleyways reveals the true charm of this seaport village. Weathered shingles, and lively gardens go hand in hand.

Lobsterfest (above)

Homemade clam *chowdah*, fresh boiled lobster, and mouth-watering corn on the cob are all on the menu at the annual Rockport Rotary Club's Lobsterfest. The event is held each year at the American Legion Hall and benefits the club's scholarship fund as well as many community projects.

Sidewalk Art (left)

Chalk it up to Motif #1 for inspiring artists of all mediums. The small fishing shack on Bradley Wharf has been deemed the most painted and photographed building in the nation. Rockport remains an important contributor to American art, with artists gathering here to capture her beauty since the first art studio was established in 1873.

Fresh and Tasty *(above and right)*

For the freshest seafood on the planet, the Roy Moore Lobster Company on Bearskin Neck is the place to be. But don't expect any fancy waiters or fine linen tablecloths—this is seafood "in the rough," the way it ought to be. Just stroll on in to this tiny establishment and order up. You can sit out back and enjoy it while overlooking the harbor.

Sewall-Scripture House *(above)*

To tour the Seawall-Scripture House is to take a walk back in time. Furnishings and artifacts depict life in the 1800s. The home is decorated with paintings from notable Cape Ann artists such as Fitz Henry (Hugh) Lane and Aldro T. Hibbard. The museum is owned and operated by the Sandy Bay Historical Society and is open from mid-June to mid-September.

Autumn in Rockport *(left)*

Rockport shops and restaurants herald in the fall season with colorful displays of pumpkins, gourds, and mums by the basketful. The colors of autumn are summers encore before settling into a long white winter.

Shalin Liu Performance Center

(above and right)

A spectacular addition to downtown Rockport, the Shalin Liu Performance Center is home to Rockport Music and the Rockport Chamber Music Festival. World-renowned artists perform in an intimate setting with the Atlantic Ocean as their backdrop. It is a stunning venue whose design is in perfect harmony with its Main Street neighbors.

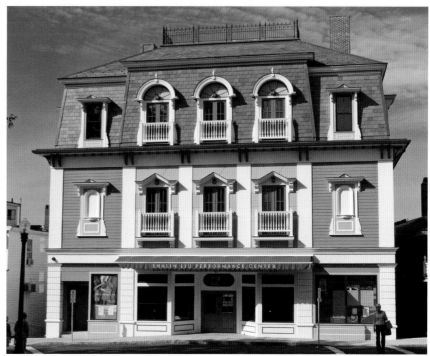

Scuba Class *(opposite top)*

Lobsters, striped bass, star fish, flounder, scampering crabs, and spiny sea urchins are some of the wonders of the deep that wait to be discovered by a local scuba diving class. Coastal Cape Ann draws scuba enthusiasts from all over. Classes and excursions are offered by several dive shops throughout the area.

A Gathering of Artists *(opposite bottom)*

Established in 1921 in the studio of Aldro T. Hibbard, the Rockport Art Association has grown to nearly 250 members and 800 contributing artists. One of the oldest organizations in the country, it provides exhibits, classes, lectures, and demonstrations. The museum's collection is a wonderful depiction of life on Cape Ann.

Pigeon Cove *(above)*

An inspiration to artists and writers who often visited here, Pigeon Cove boasts a rocky coastline that is immersed in natural beauty. Henry David Thoreau and Ralph Waldo Emerson frequented the area. The impressive Ralph Waldo Emerson Inn, overlooking the vast Atlantic Ocean was named for the famous author who often stayed there.

Pebble Beach *(above)*

Smoothed by the constant movement of the ocean, stones of various colors and shapes are layered over the long stretch of sand that is aptly named Pebble Beach. The rocky reef just offshore make this a favorite spot for scuba divers. The beach is located on Penzance Road and parking is free.

Twin Lights *(left and opposite)*

Thacher Island features two 124-foot-tall granite towers that mark a dangerous area of coastline just off of Cape Ann. Located on either end of an island spanning some 50 acres, they are the only operating twin lighthouses in the country. Open to the public, the Cape Ann Light Station was designated a National Historic Landmark in 2001.

Scenic Cruise *(opposite)*

A gentle wind guides this couple along a tour of Choate Island (also known as Hog Island). Overseen by The Trustees of Reservations, the island, with its dark pine forest and historic Choate Farm, is a nature lover's paradise. It is part of over 700 acres of small islands and salt marshes that make up the Cornelius and Miné S. Crane Wildlife Refuge.

Row Boats *(above)*

A pair of row boats bob in still waters, awaiting their next excursion. Whether rowing for pleasure or preparing for the annual 6-mile Essex River Race, the Essex River has some of the most scenic views on Cape Ann.

Essex Marsh

Nature, at times, paints in the abstract as expressed here in the flowing lines of a tidal marsh. Cape Ann is blessed with a unique and stunning environment for outdoor recreation thanks to the Essex County Greenbelt Association, an organization dedicated to preserving rivers, salt marshes, and wildlife corridors throughout Cape Ann.

A Rich Cape Ann Palette

A sunny dory is moored harmoniously in an Essex marsh of golden grasses. There are as many different types of dories as there are New England towns. Sailing dories became popular pleasure craft after the demand for working dories decreased at the start of the 20th century.

Art in the Barn *(above and left)*

Each summer in June, the barns at the Cox Reservation are transformed with a massive collection of paintings, sculptures, crafts, and jewelry created by dozens of regional artists. The weekend event includes the exhibition and sale, as well as a wine and cheese reception. Art in the Barn benefits the Essex County Greenbelt Association.

Family of Boat Builders *(above and right)*

Boat building is synonymous with the town of Essex and the Burnham family has been designing boats here since the early 1800s. H. A. Burnham Boat Building and Design continues a ship-building tradition that has been passed down from generation to generation, launching some 4,000 exquisite schooners since its beginnings.

Serenity *(above)*

Acres of woodland and pristine marshes are indicative of Essex. The Chebacco boat in the foreground, *Lewis H. Story*, was commissioned by the Essex Ship-building Museum and built by H. A. Burnham Boat Building and Design. It was named for Essex shipwright and maritime historian, Lewis H. Story, who was born in 1873.

Anchors Away *(left)*

A crowd gathers on a calm summer evening to witness a much anticipated boat launch along the Essex River Basin. Masterful craftsmen have passed down valuable shipbuilding techniques from generation to generation. More two-masted, wooden fishing schooners have been built in Essex than anywhere else in the world.

Essex Farmhouse

The simple beauty of an old farmhouse reflected in a still river often prompts passersby to stop and admire it. It remains a favorite subject for artists to capture on canvas. This gray, weathered structure along Route 133 is the view that the many patrons of J .T. Farnham's enjoy while dining on their favorite fried clams or lobster roll.

Kayaking Conomo Point (*opposite*)

A lone kayaker dips his paddle into a river of gold. The day is winding down in this small clamming town and the spit of land jutting into Essex Bay called Conomo Point has, once again, offered up one of the most amazing sunsets on earth. Summer residents enjoy the view from the front porches of charming cottages found all along the point.

Shades of Autumn (*top and bottom*)

With bursts of red, yellow, and gold, birches, elms, and oaks paint a changing scene along lakefronts and front yards as summer fades into autumn. Crisp blue skies and cooler air usher in the fall season that also includes a harvest of delectable locally-grown fruits and vegetables.

Down on the Farm *(above)*

The Town of Essex has a rich agricultural history dating back to its colonial beginnings. Along with maritime industry and clamming, farms have contributed greatly to the development and character of Cape Ann. Picturesque farmhouses nestled in wide open pastures can be seen along winding roads that meander through the town.

Cogswell's Grant *(opposite top)*

Bertram K. and Nina Fletcher Little purchased this colonial farmhouse in 1937 and continued to restore it and to fill it with American folk art for the next sixty years. From painted furniture to hooked rugs and weathervanes, lovers of early American antiques can visit the unique and even quirky collection at Cogswell's Grant from June to October.

Main Street *(opposite bottom)*

Main Street in Essex is lined with quaint structures, rich in color, that house antique shops, restaurants, and private homes. Essex has a number of antique shops where you can browse everything from high-end furnishings to heirloom jewelry. It's is a favorite antique spot on Cape Ann.

Chebacco Lake *(top)*

Children make the most of their summer vacation by dipping into the clear cool water of Chebacco Lake. This huge glistening lake, surrounded by woods, borders the towns of Essex and Hamilton. It is a hidden recreational treasure. A lake with a history, ice was once harvested here to be used in ice boxes in the days before refrigerators.

Centennial Grove *(bottom)*

Hosting summer camps as well as the annual Essex Music Festival, Centennial Grove spans some 41 acres on Chebacco Lake. The grove cottage was recently renovated and used as the setting for the movie *Grown Ups* that starred comedian Adam Sandler.

Crane Beach

Managed by the Trustees of Reservations, Crane Beach is one of Cape Ann's finest recreation areas. Part of the Bay Circuit Trail, hikers enjoy walking along the more than five miles of trails that lead through sand dunes and salt marshes. The wide span of beachfront affords spectacular views of both Ipswich Bay and Essex River Estuary.

Seafood at its Finest *(above)*

Since 1914, Woodman's has been serving up the best that Cape Ann has to offer—in the rough. Succulent fried clams, sweet lobster, tender steamers, and creamy clam *chowdah* keep them coming back for more. The iconic eatery has been inducted into the Massachusetts Restaurant Hall of Fame

Kayaks and Clammers *(left)*

By skiff or by kayak, Essex clam flats conceal this small town's true treasure just below the surface. Some of the most hard-working men on Cape Ann, clammers work in tandem with the rhythm of the tides, harvesting tons of the sweet delicacy every year. Strict regulations are monitored by the Essex Shellfish Constable.

Essex River Race

The Essex River Race begins at Route 133 in Essex, and continues out among the beaches of Ipswich, around Cross Island and back again. Kayaks and paddle boats of every kind partake in the 5.5 mile event while enjoying scenic beauty and taking on challenging currents.

Westerhoff Antiques (above)

Essex is the antique capital of the world and those who visit Alexander Westerhoff Antiques will find an exclusive inventory of rare American and European pieces including period furnishings, original paintings, ornate tapestries, and more. Located in a former church—an Essex landmark—the shop fills 4500 square feet with exquisite treasures.

Flying Dragon (left)

Howard's Flying Dragon Antiques on Main Street is brimming with collectables. Nautical, musical, agricultural, sporting—antique lovers can find goods of all kinds from days gone by. Family owned for over 30 years, Howard's is known for it's quirky messages spelled out in large gold letters in their front windows.

White Elephant Shop *(above and right)*

Got antiques? The White Elephant certainly does. Trinkets by the trunkload spill out onto the sidewalk and beckon passersby to spend hours browsing for that perfect find. From turn-of-the-century farming tools to vintage pocket watches—even the kitchen sink! The White Elephant has two locations on Route 133.

Tuck's Point *(top and bottom)*

Sailboats moor at the beautiful and busy inlet at Tuck's Point in Manchester-by-the-Sea. Tuck's Point is home to the Manchester Yacht Club, which was established in 1895. Also located here is the Manchester Sailing Association, an organization offering sailing lessons and whose racing teams partake in regattas throughout New England.

Rotunda at Tucks Point *(opposite)*

The iconic, red-roofed rotunda at Tuck's Point is a structure that has become synonymous with Manchester-by-the-Sea. This romantic setting is often rented out for weddings and gatherings of all kinds. The park includes a small beach, playground, picnic tables, and The Chowder House, a small covered function area.

Blackburn Challenge Contenders *(top)*

For now, this rowing duo safely practices in serene waters, but strong wind and rough surf await them at the Blackburn Challenge. Circling all of Cape Ann for more than 20 miles, the race draws hundreds of the area's hardiest rowers. It's a demanding competition, held out in open waters, and is only for the most experienced seafarers.

Outter Harbor *(bottom)*

Sightseers enjoy a tour of the town from a different point of view. Huge, stately homes on rocky foundations return the friendly gaze. Established in 1645, and renamed "Manchester-by-the-Sea" in 1990, her beautiful coastal mansions made this a favorite destination for wealthy Boston socialites in the summer.

Manchester Marine *(opposite)*

Since the late 1800s, boat yards of Manchester-by-the-Sea have built many large vessels from racing sloops to the 110-foot, wooden "subchasers" used during WWII. Today, Manchester Marine is a full-service yacht yard and boat storage facility, specializing in the updating of classic yachts with the very latest in sailing technology.

Land and Water *(top and bottom)*

Hints of Colonial America can be found in the architectural styles of historic homes throughout Manchester-by-the-Sea. A walk along these small-town roads will yield everything from steep, well-kept A-frames, homes of sturdy granite, or a typical quaint clapboard-style dwellings.

Gliding Along the Marshes *(opposite top)*

Heading up the creek from the harbor, a paddleboarder glides quietly along, taking in the sights and sounds of the rich, natural habitat that Masconomo Park has to offer.

Historic Waterways *(opposite bottom)*

Reflections of lush summer surroundings afford a tranquil view for those along this granite-lined waterway that runs from Central Pond into the harbor next to the Old Firehouse.

Painted Turret

Queen-Ann-style architecture can be found throughout Cape Ann. Many Colonial American structures sport Victorian details with painted turrets and shingles fashioned in geometric designs. Fresh, modern colors paint a new face on a well-preserved architectural treasure.

Small Town America

There is nothing more welcoming than the simplicity of a covered porch surrounded by heaps of summer blooms. Quaint and friendly houses like these are the hallmark of a small Cape Ann town.

Historic Architecture

(opposite top and bottom)

From a creative vantage point, Colonial American architecture takes on a modern art appeal. Sunny yellows help to shed the winter blues, and welcoming front porches invite neighbors to come and sit a while.

Head of the Harbor (top)

Framed by seaside park greenery, fishing boats moored in tranquil waters create a picture-postcard scene. Fishing was the dominant livelihood in Manchester-by-the-Sea during the early 1800s, but by mid-century, the town was becoming a seasonal resort. Presidents, princes, and many distinguished Bostonians summered here.

Baker's Island Ferry (bottom)

The water shuttle, *Double Eagle,* takes residents and their visitors to and from the mainland from Baker's Island. Approximately 5 miles off shore, Baker's Island is a private summer retreat with more than 50 cottages and a lighthouse. The lighthouse is owned and maintained by the Essex National Heritage Commission.

Bird Watching

A gathering of bird watchers also take in dramatic ocean views at Coolidge Reservation. Coolidge Reservation includes 66 acres of varied natural habitats including rocky coastline, salt marshes, woodlands, a sandy beach, and a wide grassy Ocean Lawn overlooking the ocean. The area supports a variety of birds and wildlife.

Capt. Cyrus Dodge House *(top)*

Manchester-by-the-Sea was once a thriving fishing village, where dozens of sea captains and their families settled. Period homes like these can be found throughout the town's historic district, which was added to the National Register of Historic Places in 1990.

Manchester Historical Society *(bottom)*

Built in 1823, the Trask House was once a general store run by Abigail Hooper. She married, Richard Trask, one of the town's most successful sea captains, and continued a successful decades-long entrepreneurship. Today, the museum is home to the Manchester Historical Society, where visitors can enjoy free guided tours.

Manchester Library *(opposite)*

Established in 1887, this impressive structure of New England ashlar stone was designed by Charles F. McKim. Initially, the building was part library, part headquarters for the Grand Army of the Republic, and part Civil War Memorial. The library has since added a childrens' room, and now has an extensive online catalog.

No.1 Firehouse Museum (above)

This restored 19th-century firehouse museum contains period artifacts from both police and fire departments. Also housed here are two antique fire engines—the *Seaside No. 2*, an early 1900s, horse-drawn steam pumper, and the *Torrent*, an early 1800s hand pumper. Admission is free during July and August.

Masconomo Park (opposite top and bottom)

Park benches along the water's edge provide a serene resting spot in Masconomo Park. The park also includes a playground, a baseball field, and a bandstand. Originally named Jeffrey's Creek in 1636, Manchester-by-the-Sea was once inhabited by the Agawam Indian tribe, who's chief was called *Masconomo*.

The Old Pier *(above)*

Barnacle-covered remnants of an old pier are testimony to nature's harsh demands. Ceaseless waves, like the second hand of a clock, mark the passing of time and eventually prove no match for man-made structures.

Commuter Rail *(right)*

The beautiful towns of Cape Ann make up some of the most desirable bedroom communities on the North Shore. The MBTA commuter rail provides convenient access to and from the Boston area, whether a busy executive heading to work, or a visitor seeking respite from busy city life.

Singing Beach at Dawn *(opposite)*

Soft and vibrant, dawn breaks to reveal the beauty of Singing Beach. The beach is named for the mysterious whistling sound that emanates from moving sand. Each day brings a new appreciation for the immeasurable beauty and individual character of Gloucester, Rockport, Essex, and Manchester-by-the-Sea—our beautiful Cape Ann.

Alan Murtagh

I have always considered myself to be fortunate as a photographer, as I have lived, surrounded by beautiful scenery in New Zealand, British Columbia, and Oregon.

Even as an experienced, award-winning photographer, I did not have a full appreciation of the term "quality of light" until I moved to Cape Ann. The range and diversity of both ever-changing seasonal light, and subject matter, make this area an artist's heaven. And it is those attractions that make producing a fresh new book illustrating this area not as simple a task as might be first thought, as it has all been done before by some very famous and talented photographers, painters, and other artists.

I have tried to show some of the most popular attractions of this area from a fresh and interesting new viewpoint, and hope that I have succeeded in piquing the viewer's interest.

This book is not about my photography. It is about Cape Ann, and the people who live here; people with the same rich diversity of background and character as the scenery, light, and subjects.

I would like to thank those people who welcomed me into their homes, places of business, and their lives, to allow me to show the true character of this beautiful area.

Although my images are published in four other publications, this is my first solo book.

More of my work may be seen at my website, at: http://stockstills.ifp3.com.